WHOSE POO?

FUSION

I0795433

POO IN THE CITY

by
John Wood

BEARPORT PUBLISHING
Minneapolis, Minnesota

Credits:
All images are courtesy of Shutterstock.com, unless otherwise specified. With thanks to Getty Images, Thinkstock Photo, and iStockphoto.

Front Cover – Nynke van Holten, Ico Maker, avian. Title typeface used throughout – PremiumVector. Vector flies – Top Vector Studio. 2 – Andrea Izzotti. 4–5 – Natursports, Irina Kryvets, tynyuk. 6–7 – RudenkoStudio, stockphoto mania, supasart meekumrai, HYLE, Net Vector. 8–9 – PauliusPeleckis, Alfmaler, StockSmartStart, Pixie Image, GoodStudio. 10–11 – Bespaliy, DiamondGT, Bob Deering, Nynke van Holten, 5 second Studio. 12–13 – Maksym Fesenko, TanitaKo, ivector, Banana Walking, Kastoluza. 14–15 – Mikheeva Art, Marti Bug Catcher, Eric Isselee, Andrea Izzotti, yusufdemirci, Ekaterina V. Borisova. 16–17 – Jakub Rutkiewicz, bardzo.photo, ChingizDs. 18–19 – Jay Ondreicka, Jim Cumming, Kirsanov Valeriy Vladimirovich, Eric Isselee, BlueRingMedia. 20–21 – Bilal Kocabas, Milan Rybar, Rumka vodki, Nora Hachio, baldezh. 22–23 – Doug McLean, Al-Tair, Panimoni, Girts Ragelis, CuteCharacters, Lili Kudrili.

Bearport Publishing Company Product Development Team
Publisher: Jen Jenson; Director of Product Development: Spencer Brinker; Managing Editor: Allison Juda; Editor: Cole Nelson; Associate Editor: Naomi Reich; Associate Editor: Tiana Tran; Art Director: Colin O'Dea; Designer: Kim Jones; Designer: Kayla Eggert; Product Development Specialist: Owen Hamlin

Library of Congress Cataloging-in-Publication Data is available at www.loc.gov or upon request from the publisher.

ISBN: 979-8-89232-749-7 (hardcover)
ISBN: 979-8-89232-799-2 (paperback)
ISBN: 979-8-89232-836-4 (ebook)

For more information, write to Bearport Publishing, 5357 Penn Avenue South, Minneapolis, MN 55419.

CONTENTS

ALL ABOUT POO

If you think you are safe from animal poo in the city, you're wrong! Poo is everywhere in cities. Let's find out which animals do the smelly deed.

Don't touch any poo you find in the city. Poo has lots of nasty things in it!

On the next pages, you will see poo that has been left in the city. Learn about the poo, and choose which animal you think made it. Then, turn the page to see if you were right!

SPLAT SCAT

Look at that car. It is covered with poo! Who dropped it here?

Whose poo could this be? Choose which of these three animals you think did it.

You think I made that mess?

Raccoon

Cockroach

Pigeon

The poo smells funny. It smells kind of sour.

WHOSE POO WAS IT?

Pigeons are **omnivores**. They eat mostly seeds and grains, but they also munch on bugs. Pigeons in the city will eat almost anything, including human food.

Pigeons poo and pee from the same hole in their bodies. It is called a cloaca (klo-AY-kuh). The white part of their droppings is pee and the dark part is poo.

Pigeon droppings have lots of **acid** in them. This causes the sour smell.

Pigeon poo can **erode** metal and stone over time.

LITTLE LOGS

There is poo on the sidewalk.
Which animal left it behind?

Whose poo do you think it is? Choose from these three animals.

The poo is kind of hidden. Maybe the animal does not want anyone to find it.

WHOSE POO WAS IT?

Cats often hide their poo. They do this to avoid attracting bigger, scarier animals.

Cats are **predators**. They hunt and eat other animals, such as mice, rats, rabbits, and birds. Cat owners may also feed their pets cat food.

Cat poo smells bad because of all the meat in a cat's **diet**.

Cats are most active in the morning and in the evening. If they are outdoors, this is when they hunt.

SNEAKY SQUIRTS

What an interesting-looking poo!
What animal could have done this?

These droppings are very dark. They are tube-shaped and a little pointy at the ends.

The poo is full of berries. There may also be small bones and bits of fur inside. This tells us a lot about what the animal ate.

Whose poo could this be? Choose which of these three animals you think did it.

It stinks! The smell is much stronger than that from most other poo.

WHOSE POO WAS IT?

Foxes eat a bit of everything. They hunt small animals, such as **rodents**, birds, and frogs. But they also eat seeds, berries, and fruit.

Foxes are awake mostly at night. In addition to hunting, they also go **scavenging**. This means they go searching for any food they can find. Foxes may snack on trash or animals that are already dead.

Foxes make noises that sound similar to human screams. They do this to scare away predators.

POOEY PELLETS

What have we found inside this building? It's another poo! But who did it?

These **pellets** are found in groups. They look dark brown and shiny.

The pellets are small. They are shaped a bit like jelly beans.

Which of these three animals do you think did this poo?

There are chewed up pieces of the wall near the poo. What animal would do that?

WHOSE POO WAS IT?

It was the rat's POO!

Rats will eat almost anything. They chow down on seeds and grains, but they also eat meat, plants, eggs, and trash.

Rats can poo up to 50 pellets each day.

Rats are very good climbers. They can easily climb up flat walls.

At first, a rat's poo is shiny and black. It becomes dustier and gray as it gets older.

BONUS POO!

TIMELESS TOILETING

Ducks **digest** their food very quickly. This means they poo often.

Ducklings may poo as often as every 10 minutes.

COLORFUL POOS

Some people keep bee hives in the city. But did you know that bees poo, too? Their droppings are sticky and bright yellow or orange.

Asian honeybees rub other animals' poo on their hives. This keeps killer hornets away.

GLOSSARY

acid a substance that can be dangerous and cause harm

diet the foods that a person or animal usually eats

digest to break down food into things that can be used by the body

erode to slowly wear down over time

omnivores animals that eat both plants and animals

pellets small, hard balls of poop or undigested food

predators animals that hunt and eat other animals

rodents animals, such as rats and mice, that have four feet and long front teeth

scavenging searching for food from things that have been thrown away

INDEX